FARM ANIMALS

GOATS

Ann Larkin Hansen
ABDO Publishing Company

visit us at
www.abdopub.com

Published by Abdo Publishing Company 4940 Viking Drive, Edina, Minnesota 55435.
Copyright © 1998 by Abdo Consulting Group, Inc. International copyrights reserved in
all countries. No part of this book may be reproduced in any form without written
permission from the publisher.

Printed in the United States.

Cover Photo credits: Peter Arnold, Inc.
Interior Photo credits: Peter Arnold, Inc.

Edited by Lori Kinstad Pupeza

Library of Congress Cataloging-in-Publication Data

Hansen, Ann Larkin.
    Goats / Ann Larkin Hansen.
    p. cm. -- (Farm animals)
    Includes index.
    Summary: An overview of the most playful and affectionate of all farm animals.
    ISBN 1-56239-604-8
    1. Goats--Juvenile literature. [1. Goats.] I. Title. II. Series: Hansen, Ann
Larkin. Farm animals.
    SF383.35.H35 1998
    636.3'9--dc20

    96-3803
    CIP
    AC

About the Author
Ann Larkin Hansen has a degree in history from the University of St. Thomas
in St. Paul, Minnesota. She currently lives with her husband and three boys
on a farm in northern Wisconsin, where they raise beef cattle, chickens, and
assorted other animals.

Contents

Born to Climb

Goats are always going up. They like to climb rocks and mountains. They like to sleep above the ground on benches or platforms. They like to reach up to eat leaves and bark instead of down for grass. They like to climb up and over things.

Around the world, more people drink goat milk than cow milk. Every place that it is too hot, dry, or steep for cows, you will find goats.

Opposite page: Goats like to climb on top of stuff.

How Goats Were Tamed

About 10,000 years ago, people in the Middle East first began to milk goats instead of only hunting them for meat. They discovered how to make butter, cheese, and yogurt from the milk.

These early **goatherders** also found that goats were as friendly and as smart as dogs. The goats ate thorns and brush, which cleared new land. Goats became known as the "friend of the pioneer."

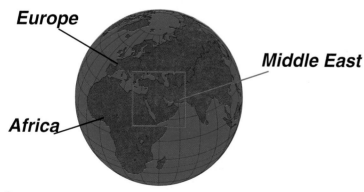

Europe

Middle East

Africa

A goat feeding
on leaves

How Goats Behave

Goats are the most playful and affectionate of all farm animals. But they need a routine—everything happening in the same way at the same time every day. Goats hate to be alone, and they are famous for being able to open gates and latches with their mouths.

Goats can't be herded, they must be led. They will only follow someone they know and trust. In the wild, a **herd** of goats follows its **king buck** and **queen doe**. On a farm, they follow the **goatherd**.

Opposite page: Goats
near a barn

How a Goat Eats and Climbs

Goats learn from other goats what is good to eat and how to climb.

Goats have slanted hooves that don't slip on rocks and dirt. They can climb places no other animal can go. Their mouths are so tough that goats can

Goats have four stomachs.

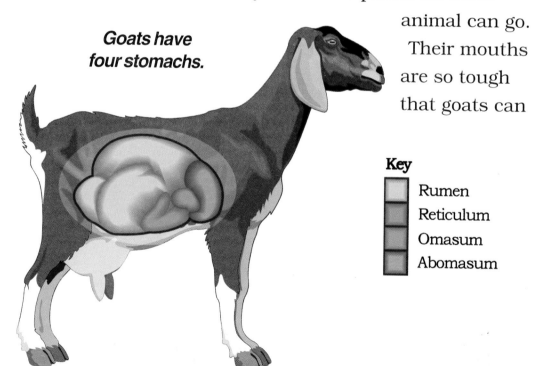

Key

- Rumen
- Reticulum
- Omasum
- Abomasum

eat thorns. After a goat has filled its first stomach with food, it lays down and burps some of it back up. The goat chews this **cud** thoroughly then swallows it down to the next three stomachs. All four-stomached cud-chewing animals are called **ruminants**.

A mountain goat in the Rocky Mountains.

What Goats Look Like

Most goats are born with horns, but most goatkeepers remove them. This way the goat can't get its head tangled in a fence, hurt other goats, or hurt the goatkeeper. Adult **does**, the females, weigh about 150 pounds (68 kilograms), and **bucks**, the males, weigh about 200 pounds (90 kilograms).

Like cows and sheep, goats have no upper front teeth. The bucks grow beards, and many goats have **wattles**. These are pieces of skin that hang below a goat's chin. The hair of some goats, like the Angora, is long and fine enough to make beautiful cloth.

Opposite page: Goats are born with horns.

Types of Goats

In the United States, most goats are **dairy goats**. They make milk for people who are allergic to cow's milk, or who just like goat's milk better! A dairy goat has a large **udder** where milk is made, and two **teats**.

In the southwestern states, and other parts of the world, meat goats are also raised. In the Himalaya mountains Kashmir and Cheghu goats are kept for their hair, which is made into rugs and tents.

Opposite page:
Domestic goat kids

Caring for Goats

Goats are picky eaters and cannot stand to be wet. Their shed must be well-bedded and dry, and a sleeping bench is nice. The shed must also be well-built so the goats can't tear it apart.

Goats do not need much grain. They will not eat moldy or dusty hay, and they will not eat hay off the ground. They must have plenty of rough, clean feed to stay warm and healthy. There must always be clean water and salt available.

Opposite page:
Young goats on a
farm in Idaho.

Grazing Goats

Because goats are such good climbers and jumpers, pasture fences must be high and tight.

Goats need a special sort of pasture. They do not eat grass and clover like other farm animals. They like bushes, and nettles, and all sorts of weeds and brush. Goats use land that is good for nothing else.

Opposite page: Goats need to be fenced in because they are such good climbers.

Keeping Goats Healthy

Goats do not get sick much. If they get wet or chilled, they may get **pneumonia**, and must be carefully nursed. Sometimes goats get little pockets of infection, called **abscesses**. These must be lanced and drained.

Dairy goats must be **vaccinated** against **tuberculosis** and other diseases that humans can catch. Sometimes goats need medicine to kill worms that live in their stomachs. Goats' hooves need to be trimmed regularly, just like your fingernails.

Opposite page: Goats can catch many of the same diseases that humans can.

Baby Goats

A **doe** goat is pregnant for five months. When she is ready to kid—to have her babies—she needs a pen that is warm, dry, and private. Does will have one to five **kids**, but two is usual.

Goat kids are fun! They are active, curious, and friendly. They will chew on almost anything, and get into all sorts of mischief. The **goatherd** must watch them carefully.

Opposite page:
Angora goat with kid,
from Turkey.

Growing Up

After a few days, the **kids** are put in a pen away from their mothers so milking can begin. The kids are fed several times a day from pans or bottles. By the time they are one week old, they begin to nibble on hay.

As the kids grow and their stomachs develop, they drink less milk and eat more hay. When they are eight to ten weeks old, they are **weaned** from milk and fed only hay and grain. By the time they are seven or eight months, they are ready to join the adults.

Opposite page: Young goats drink milk at first, but soon begin to eat more and more hay.

Dairying

As soon as the **kids** are born, the **does** start to give milk. Every morning and every evening the **goatherd** milks the does. The doe jumps up on the milking stand so the milker does not have to bend over so far.

A doe will produce 125 to 200 gallons (473 to 757 liters) of milk in 10 months. Then she has two months off before she kids again. All the milking equipment must be very clean to keep the milk fresh and good-tasting.

Opposite page: A doe can produce as much as 200 gallons (757 liters) of milk in 10 months.

Glossary

Abscess—a pocket of infection, soft and filled with pus.

Browse—to eat leaves, weeds, bark, and brambles.

Buck—an adult male goat.

Cud—partially digested food that is burped up and further chewed by the goat before being swallowed for final digestion.

Dairy goat—a goat that makes milk for human consumption.

Doe—an adult female goat.

Goatherd—a person who keeps goats.

Herd—a group of goats, or moving a group of animals in a bunch by driving them from behind.

Kid—a baby goat.

Kidding—a doe giving birth is said to be kidding.

King buck—the head buck in a goat herd.

Pneumonia—infection of the lungs to which goats are susceptible.

Queen doe—the head female in a goat herd.

Ruminant—any four-stomached, cud-chewing animal.

Teat—the elongated nipples on the udder. Milk comes out of the teats.

Tuberculosis—a dangerous disease of the lungs.

Udder—the bag-like organ between the hind legs that holds the milk.

Vaccinate—to give a shot to stop sickness.

Wattles—hair-covered skin tags that hang below the chin on some goats.

Wean—to quit feeding milk.

Internet Sites

The Virtual Farm
http://www.manawatu.gen.nz/~tiros/ftour1.htm
A very impressive display including photos and sound. This
site is all about dairy farming in New Zealand.

Museums in the Classroom
**http://www.museum.state.il.us/mic_home/newton/
project/**
Prairie Chickens and the prairie in Illinois by Mrs.
Vanderhoof's third grade class and Mrs. Volk's fourth grade
science classes.

Goats
http://www.ics.uci.edu/~pazzani/4H/Goats.html
This site has photos, graphics, and sound. It has tons of
information on raising goats and it even has a goat game.

Virtual Pig Dissection
http://mail.fkchs.sad27.k12.me.us/fkchs/vpig/
Learn how to dissect a pig without hurting a pig. This is a
really cool site that gets a lot of traffic.

Sheep
http://www.ics.uci.edu/~pazzani/4H/Sheep.html
This site has everything you would want to know about sheep. Why raising sheep is fun, the sounds sheep make, sheep statistics, basic care, sheep supplies, and much more.

Castalia Llamas
http://www.rockisland.com/~castalia/cllama.html
Chosen as a hotsite, featured on TV, listed in Popular Science's WebWatch. Full of llama facts, images and stories to amuse and bewilder. This is a cool site, check it out.

These sites are subject to change. Go to your favorite search engine and type in "farm animals" for more sites.

PASS IT ON
Tell Others What You Like About Animals!
To educate readers around the country, pass on interesting tips about animals, maybe a fun story about your animal or pet, and little-known facts about animals. We want to hear from you!
To get posted on ABDO Publishings website, E-mail us at "animals@abdopub.com"

Index